To John and Gill McLay

All rights reserved. Published by Scholastic Inc., *Publishers since 1920*, by arrangement with David Fickling Books, Oxford, England.
SCHOLASTIC and associated logos are trademarks and/or registered trademarks of Scholastic Inc. DAVID FICKLING BOOKS
and associated logos are trademarks and/or registered trademarks of David Fickling Books.
First published in the United Kingdom in 2019 by David Fickling Books, 31 Beaumont Street, Oxford OX1 2NP as *Lesser Spotted Animals 2*.
www.davidficklingbooks.com
The publisher does not have any control over and does not assume any responsibility for author or third-party websites or their content.

Library of Congress Cataloging-in-Publication Data available

ISBN 978-1-338-34961-0
10 9 8 7 6 5 4 3 2 1   19 20 21 22 23
Printed in China

First edition, August 2019

Book design by Becky Chilcott

EVEN MORE LESSER SPOTTED ANIMALS

MORE BRILLIANT BEASTS YOU NEVER KNEW YOU NEEDED TO KNOW ABOUT

BOO!

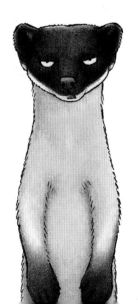

David Fickling Books

Scholastic Inc. · New York

Martin Brown

CONTENTS

HMMF!

INTRODUCTION

TUFTED PYGMY
SQUIRREL

WHAT'S YOUR FAVORITE MONKEY? WHICH BAT IS BEST? IS one antelope more appealing than another? Of the twenty species of kangaroo rat, which do you prefer? What are your top ten squirrels?

Not sure? It's not surprising. There are thousands of different types of wild animal out there, each one with a name and a story all of its own. However, it seems that the only ones we hear about are the same famous few big-name animals — the elephants and zebras, the polar bears and pandas — animals with names that are so big there's no room for anything else. Until now . . .

SPOTTED
SOUSLIK

KINTAMPO ROPE
SQUIRREL

PREVOST'S
SQUIRREL

Welcome to *Even More Lesser Spotted Animals*. Just as *Lesser Spotted Animals* showed you some of the wonderfully wow wildlife we never get to see, this book tells the tales of even more of the world's unseen and unsung creatures. Creatures whose unfamiliar names have just as much right to be heard as the big names of the animal "A" list.

Take those big-name, bigwig, big cats for example. Lions fill our picture books. Tigers are always on TV. Jaguars have become cars and Pumas are shoes. They're all over the place! Just like their famous, big-name animal friends. So much so that when we think of animals we think of the BIG names — and *only* the big names. Then, when we think of nature conservation and saving animals, we think "save the panda, save the jaguar." What about all the others? There are roughly

ABERT'S
SQUIRREL

UINTA
CHIPMUNK

two hundred and eighty different species of squirrel alone. And although many of them are common, some are dangerously scarce and need help to survive. But how can we help something survive if we don't even know it exists?

VANCOUVER ISLAND MARMOT

This book names the little guys so that when we think about the big wide world of wildlife, we think about *all* the animals — not just *some* of them. Endangered or everywhere, their names deserve to be known. So you won't find any king-of-the-jungle, fancy-pants lions here — we've got the magnificent maned wolf instead. No blue whales either; we've got beaked whales. And no giraffes, just gerenuks — and lorises and dingisos and dibatags and many, many more . . .

What's your favorite monkey? Read on. You might find out.

DINGISO
Teddy bear kangaroo of New Guinea

IN THE LONG LIST OF ANIMALS ADAPTED TO LIVE IN TREES you wouldn't expect to find kangaroos. They stand on two legs, they have huge back feet, and they bounce! And yet some kangaroos *do* live in trees. Unsurprisingly, they are called tree kangaroos. When climbing, their front claws grip the trunk while their powerful back legs push upward in little hops. In the branches they are agile and sure-footed, helped by rough, grippy, cushion-like pads on their feet. Coming down is easy. They either scramble down backward or they jump. A tree kangaroo can jump thirty feet down to another tree or, amazingly, twice that distance to the ground — without injury. That's three times higher than the tallest giraffe.

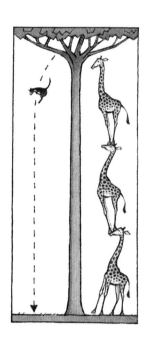

BEAR CUB

KANGAROO

The dingiso is a tree kangaroo from New Guinea and if any animal was designed to become a cuddly toy, this is it. With its thick dark fur and round face, it looks more like a bear cub than a kangaroo — and ready-made for cuddling. If approached, it rears up, lifts its arms, and whistles. The local Moni tribesmen say dingisos are ancestor spirits and this is them saying "hello." But maybe they're just getting ready for a big snuggly hug — or to scratch you to bits.

SIZE: about the size of a one-year-old toddler with a long tail

WHAT THEY EAT: leaves and fruit – probably (they have yet to be closely studied)

WHERE THEY LIVE: the forested mountains of western New Guinea, Indonesia

STATUS: endangered. The Moni people honor and protect them; others do not

AND: they are rare anyway. They were only first seen by outsiders in 1994, and very few have been seen since

FOREST MUSK DEER
China's toothy tree-leaper

IF YOU LOOKED OUT THE WINDOW AT THE SPARROWS ON THE BIRD FEEDER and saw a deer in the tree you might think that your little brother had put something in your breakfast cereal. If you then saw that the deer had fangs, you'd probably stop throttling your little brother and call an ambulance. However, if that window was in a house in the forested mountains of southern China, perhaps all would be well — because you would most likely be looking at a forest musk deer.

Musk deer are unusual creatures to say the least. They don't have antlers, but they do have long canine teeth, which stick out below their mouths in quite a fang-like manner. Behind the main hooves on each foot they have long lateral hooves that give them amazing grip — even enough to leap (rather than climb) into the branches of a tree. But perhaps their most important, and tragic, feature is what gives them their name — musk.

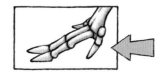

Musk is a strong-smelling waxy oil produced by the males to mark their territory and signal to the females. This earthy, sweet-smelling liquid is used for traditional Chinese medicines and the finest French perfumes. And it's as valuable as gold. So musk deer are hunted for their musk — a lot. There might have been a million forest musk deer in the 1960s. In the 1990s that number was down to fewer than 200,000. And it's *still* going down.

These days, musk deer are protected, but that hasn't stopped the poaching. The tragedy for this shy and surprising animal is that they are worth more dead than alive.

SIZE: long-legged, medium-sized dog – like a chunky whippet

WHAT THEY EAT: leaves, grasses, twigs, and lichens

WHERE THEY LIVE: patches of hillside forest from central China to northern Vietnam

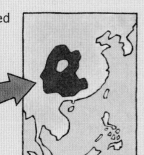

STATUS: endangered

AND: they are not true deer – and might be closer to antelopes and cattle on the family tree

NOT THAT KIND OF TREE

TWO GLIDERS
Aerial possums from eastern Australia

YOU'VE PROBABLY HEARD OF FLYING SQUIRRELS. THEY HAVE STRETCHES of loose skin at their sides between their wrists and their ankles that allow them to glide from tree to tree like furry paper planes. So that's gliding — not flying. Flying squirrels don't fly. But it's a great idea. They can quickly move around the forest and easily escape from things that want to eat them. It's such a good idea that flying squirrels aren't the only tree-dwelling mammals that do it. There are also the anomalures in Africa, the colugos in Southeast Asia, and the marsupial gliders in Australia and New Guinea.

 FLYING SQUIRREL
 ANOMALURE
 COLUGO
GLIDER

There are eight or so different types of marsupial glider — here are two of them:

YELLOW-BELLIED GLIDER: Like most marsupials, the female yellow-bellied glider has a pouch where her baby sits snugly for the first few months of its life — even when she's doing one of her 328-foot glides. The trees they depend upon for food and shelter are very tall. Getting from one to another would be a long climb down and a long climb back up again. When the baby gets bigger, it waits for Mom high in its tree-hollow home.

SIZE: as big as a skinny rabbit

WHAT THEY EAT: flower nectar, tree sap, pollen, grubs, and insects

WHERE THEY LIVE: tall forests up and down eastern Australia

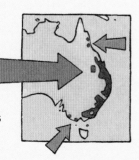

STATUS: near threatened. Some of the forests are being cut down

AND: with high screams and low gurgles they can be really noisy

SQUEERK!

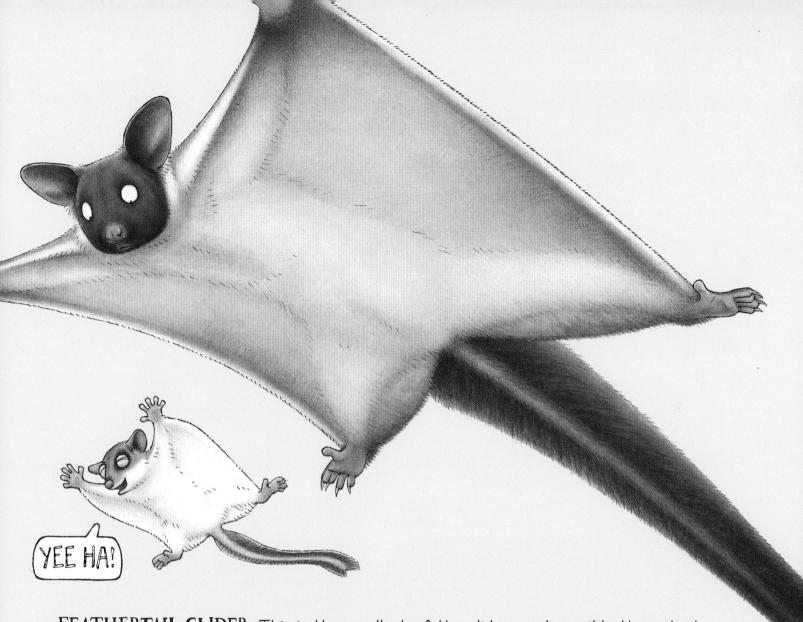

YEE HA!

FEATHERTAIL GLIDER: This is the smallest of the gliders and possibly the cutest thing in the known universe. This tiny creature has a long thin tail with long hair on the sides — like a feather. It can be used for steering and stopping when gliding — like a feather, and hanging on to twigs and branches when climbing — not like a feather.

SIZE: as big as a mouse (but cuter)

WHAT THEY EAT: nectar, pollen, fruit, and insects

WHERE THEY LIVE: different types of forest from northeastern to southeastern Australia

STATUS: least concern

AND: its fingers and toes have special pads that allow it to climb smooth and vertical surfaces

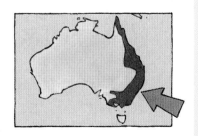

BLACK & RUFOUS SENGI

A flash of color in the African forest

THE OTHER NAME FOR THE BLACK AND RUFOUS SENGI IS THE BLACK AND rufous elephant shrew. People thought it was a sort of shrew, and because it had a long nose they said it looked a bit elephantish. But it's not a shrew and it doesn't really look like an elephant. So the local name, sengi, is used these days. So sengi it is.

WHITE-TAILED SENGI

There are between seventeen and nineteen different sengis recognized as separate species. Most are mouse- or rat-sized, but a few are as big as guinea pigs — the giant sengis. The black and rufous sengi is one of those giants. Unfortunately, not a lot is known about this dashing animal — but biologists think this giant sengi behaves a lot like the other giant sengis.

CHECKERED SENGI

All sengis stay in pairs for life but they don't really hang out together. By day they hunt for bugs and ants with their twitching, probing noses. At night they sleep tucked up in one of the several large leafy nests they've built for themselves on the ground.

GOLDEN-RUMPED SENGI

They are speedy creatures. They need to be. They can't climb trees or burrow into the earth so the only way to escape the many things that want to eat them is by running away.

For their size sengis are the fastest mammals in the world. They dash around their home territories, looking for food and visiting their nests, like tiny antelopes or pointy rabbits. But they're not antelope rabbits or shrew elephants — they are sengis. **And this dashing sengi is particularly dashing.**

GRAY-FACED SENGI

SIZE: guinea pig big

WHAT THEY EAT: insects – mostly ants and termites

WHERE THEY LIVE: dense woodland and scrub in eastern Africa

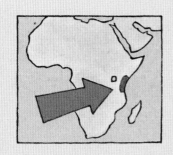

STATUS: vulnerable. Their forest habitat is being disturbed

AND: they have very long tongues that can stick out past their very long noses

THAT'S DISGUSTING

NOSE-PICKING SENGI

BLAINVILLE'S BEAKED WHALE

The marine mammal with a beak – and tusks

WHAT? WHALES HAVE BEAKS? YEP, LOTS DO. AT THE LAST COUNT, THERE were twenty-two types of beaked whales. These medium-sized whales have long, nearly toothless snouts and it's this that gives them their name. They are remarkable and mysterious creatures, but it's always the gigantic blue whale and the show-off dolphins that get all the attention. Surely a whale with a beak is worth a peek.

Beaked whales are the deep-diving, breath-holding champions of the world, often diving over half of a mile and staying under for well over an hour. It's like holding your breath for the whole time you're watching a movie. But first place goes to a Cuvier's beaked whale, which was recorded diving to nearly two miles — on one breath, which lasted an astonishing two hours and seventeen minutes!

Beaked whales dive to these great dark depths to feed on squid and deep-sea fish, which they suck into their mouths. Only the males have teeth that you can see and these are used for fighting rather than biting. Some beaked whales have their teeth at the tip of the snout, others at the sides. One has teeth that curve over the snout like straps — the strap-toothed whale.

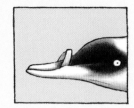

This whale — Blainville's beaked whale — has possibly the most peculiar teeth of all, sticking up, as they do, like tusks from the bulging high sides of its lower jaw. Like all beaked whales they are seldom seen and difficult to study.

Even the people who know about them don't know a lot. So if you're hoping to catch a glimpse of this whale with a beak, **don't hold your breath.**

BEAKY AND FREAKY!

SIZE: as long as two and a half men end-to-end, but as heavy as twelve

WHAT THEY EAT: fish and squid

WHERE THEY LIVE: in the warmer parts of the oceans worldwide

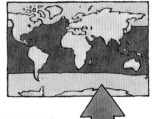

STATUS: data deficient

AND: It's named after Henri Marie Ducrotay de Blainville. Great name!

AND ANOTHER THING: the males' sticking-up teeth often have barnacles growing on them

WE'RE TOOTHBRUSHES!

HAA!

TAMANDUA
South America's treetop termite terminator

IF YOU WERE AN ANT OR A TERMITE, THE TAMANDUA WOULD BE THE THING of your nightmares. From shiny black nose to grippy tippy tail, it's an awesome insect-eating machine — or should that be monster?

It begins with a ripping crash as the walls of your home are torn away by powerful arms and terrible claws. As your soldier ants gather and you scramble to repair the damage, the tamandua tongue appears. Sickeningly sticky, with minute, backward-facing barbs, it flicks in and out twice a second. There's nowhere to run. The tongue-stuck victims are dragged into the tiny mouth and swallowed straight down to be ground to mush in the muscular stomach. Tamanduas don't need teeth. Even if your soldier ants try to fight back, they can't get past the thick fur that protects the tamandua's skin from bites and stings.

Perhaps your salvation might come from a larger predator, thinking a tamandua would make a handy snack. But first it would have to get past those fearsome claws and then deal with a spray of evil stench worse than a skunk's. The colony's only hope is that your friends don't taste very nice. So hope it's not real — that it's just a bad dream — and you didn't get a visit from . . .

SIZE: as big as a medium-sized dog – with a long tail

WHAT THEY EAT: ants and termites mostly

WHERE THEY LIVE: all sorts of forests and woodland from central Mexico to southern Brazil

STATUS: least concern

AND: their tongues can be 16 inches long – twice as long as the tamandua's head

IT'S JUST LIKE THE MOVIE

GRAY SLENDER LORIS
Little night stalker of India and Sri Lanka

LORISES ARE PRIMATES, LIKE APES, BABOONS, LEMURS – AND YOU. BUT clearly they're not like most of us. Whether we have tails or fur or long arms or sticking out noses, we are daytime animals. Lorises are creatures of the night and their features are adapted for life in the dark treetops.

They have excellent night vision due to a special reflective coating on the backs of their huge, forward-facing eyes. And a super-strong grip, thanks to extra blood vessels in their wrists and ankles, which allows them to hang on tightly for hours without getting sore muscles. They move slowly and carefully so they don't need the athletic arms and leaping legs of other primates. Hunting in the pitch-black, they inch along with pinpoint stare and gradual step, until, in a lightning grab, they snatch up their insect supper.

Slender lorises generally hunt alone, but, when the sun rises, they retreat to their favorite thicket of branches, high in a tree, to cuddle up with as many as seven others in a tangle of arms and legs called a "sleeping ball." All safe and sound.

And how safe is that? There are a few things that want to eat them, but the main threat comes from losing their forest homes and from hunting — for use in traditional medicines, or because of superstitious beliefs in their magical powers, or even for sale in the illegal pet trade.

When these little primates sense danger they freeze, stock-still, until the threat goes away. **The problem is, us big primates are not going away.**

SIZE: like a guinea pig on stilts

WHAT THEY EAT: insects mostly

WHERE THEY LIVE: tropical forest and dry scrub in southern India and Sri Lanka

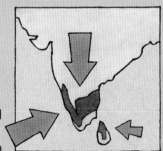

STATUS: the four types of gray slender loris are listed as either near threatened or endangered

AND: they can produce a toxic stink from patches on their upper arms to ward off predators

L'ORIS
because it's worser

24

INDIAN GIANT SQUIRREL

Big bright branch beastie

SOME ANIMAL NAMES SAY IT ALL. THE STAR-NOSED MOLE IS A MOLE WITH a nose shaped like a star; the screaming hairy armadillo is a hairy armadillo that screams; the four-horned antelope has four horns; and the least weasel is the smallest weasel of all.

 STAR-NOSED MOLE

 SCREAMING HAIRY ARMADILLO

 FOUR-HORNED ANTELOPE

 LEAST WEASEL

They don't always get it right, of course. The ferret badgers don't look much like ferrets and the tiger cat from Australia has spots — and it isn't a cat. But the Indian giant squirrel is a big squirrel from India. It's one of the biggest squirrels there is — easily twice the size of your average gray city park squirrel. It's amongst the most striking too. This one is from southern India. In different regions there are different colors: some are redder; others are a rich dark brown; and some have creamy tips to their tails.

All of them are high-flying acrobats of the forest, leaping up to twenty feet from tree to tree as they forage for food, chase intruders away, or visit one of their globe-shaped nests. These bundles of sticks and twigs are built on thin, lofty branches, strong enough to hold a nest and a squirrel but not a predator. **Indian clever squirrel.**

SIZE: as big as a small cat with an extra-long tail

WHAT THEY EAT: fruit, flowers, nuts, and bark, but also eggs and insects

WHERE THEY LIVE: upper canopy of various forest types across India

STATUS: least concern – but their numbers are going down

AND: India has lots of languages – this squirrel is called shekru in Marathi, anil in Tamil, malayannan in Malayalam, and kenjjiri in Coorgi

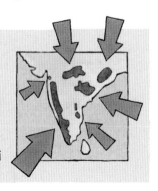

FOREST BUFFALO & RED RIVER HOG
Ears

FOREST BUFFALO

SIZE: about as big as a cow

WHAT THEY EAT: grass and occasionally leaves

WHERE THEY LIVE: western and central tropical Africa

STATUS: least concern

AND: they have swept-back horns so moving through the forest is easier

THESE TWO ANIMALS HAVE A LOT IN COMMON. THEY ARE BOTH REDDISH brown with a few black-and-white markings. They live in the same parts of Equatorial Africa. They each shelter in dense forest and emerge into clearings and marshes to graze and forage and to wallow in water holes. They are both social animals — usually hanging around in herds of three to thirty. Both are on the small side — the red river hog is the smallest wild pig in Africa and the forest buffalo is the smallest subspecies of African buffalo — half the size of its famous Cape buffalo cousin.

CAPE BUFFALO

FOREST BUFFALO

DOWN HERE

RED RIVER HOG

If we're talking about how these animals are alike, we have to say "ears." Whether for signaling or shooing flies, they make these otherwise ordinary reddish-brown beasts into creatures rather more exotic. **What a wonderful set of fab flappers they both have!**

RED RIVER HOG

SIZE: Rottweiler dog–sized pig – or piggy Rottweiler size

WHAT THEY EAT: everything

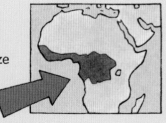

WHERE THEY LIVE: across West and Central Africa

STATUS: least concern

AND: they nose through elephant dung for undigested seeds

YUM!

THREE BATS

A few non-brown bats

IF YOU'RE AN ANIMAL THAT'S OUT ALL NIGHT AND HIDING ALL DAY YOU probably wouldn't want to be brightly colored. There are over 1,200 types of bat in the world — roughly one-fifth of all mammal species — and nearly all of them are brown or gray, but not these vivid, mouse-sized three . . .

PIED BAT: This is a quite new bat. Well, it's new to science anyway. It was only "discovered" in 2013 when one was caught in South Sudan and found to be different from the bat that scientists had thought it was. Newspapers dubbed it the panda bat — which is fine if you've never seen a panda.

WHAT THEY EAT: insects

WHERE THEY LIVE: isolated forests of central and western Africa

STATUS: vulnerable.

Only five have ever been found

AND: their scientific name, *Niumbaha*, means rare in the local language

PAINTED BAT: If you wanted a bat ready for Halloween this is it. Its orange-and-black coloring is perfect for that creepy night of pumpkins and witches. But that's as scary as they get. Unlike the flitting, quick flapping of most small bats, this bat's wing beats are slow and fluttering. More like a butterfly than a vampire.

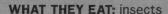

WHAT THEY EAT: insects

WHERE THEY LIVE: dry woodland in parts of India, Sri Lanka, South East Asia and Indonesia

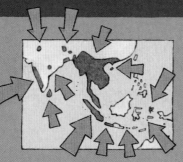

STATUS: least concern

AND: they live in small family units – just mum, dad and one or two kids

EEK!

HONDURAN WHITE BAT: This bat might be tiny but it can still build its own house. It bites along either side of the stiff central rib of a huge heliconia leaf, causing the sides of the leaf to fold down, making something like a tent. Up to twelve bats can then hang from the rib inside, hidden and safe from the sun and the rain.

WHAT THEY EAT: mostly fruit

WHERE THEY LIVE: in thick patches of lowland rain forest in Central America

STATUS: near threatened

AND: light filtering through their leaf tent makes their white fur look green – a perfect camouflage

MY TAIL IS ALSO HARD TO SEE. BECAUSE I DON'T HAVE ONE!

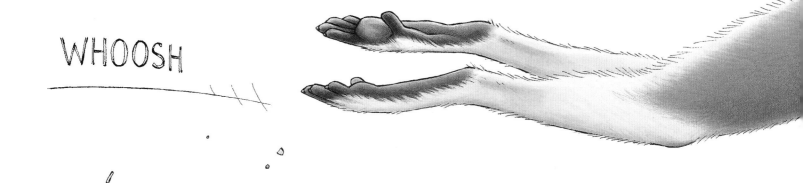

PATAS MONKEY
Red rocket of the savannah

WHOOSH

HERE COME THE MONKEYS – PATAS MONKEYS – WALKING SILENTLY between the acacia trees, flashes of orange visible through the long dry grass. There are thirty or forty of them. One is much bigger than the others — the adult male. The rest of the group are females, youngsters, and babies. They scan their surroundings constantly, checking the open savannah, the bushes where the ants gather, the sky, each other. **Always on the lookout.**

They stop. Everything seems safe. They sit and rest and begin to groom each other, picking through fur, looking for ticks and fleas. The youngsters play. There's an order here. The oldest, most important females get the best places to sit, and are groomed by the next most important members of the group. There are no other adult males around. They are off in a gang by themselves. Once they've grown up they can no longer stay with the family. There's only room for one boss male.

ME

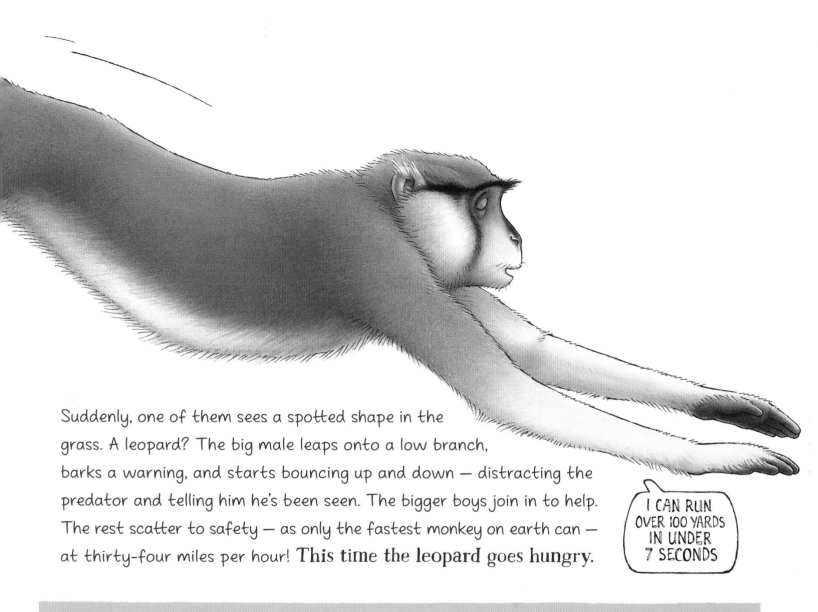

Suddenly, one of them sees a spotted shape in the grass. A leopard? The big male leaps onto a low branch, barks a warning, and starts bouncing up and down — distracting the predator and telling him he's been seen. The bigger boys join in to help. The rest scatter to safety — as only the fastest monkey on earth can — at thirty-four miles per hour! **This time the leopard goes hungry.**

I CAN RUN OVER 100 YARDS IN UNDER 7 SECONDS

SIZE: as big as a medium-sized skinny dog – another whippet

WHAT THEY EAT: ants and tree gum, but also other insects, fruits, and seeds

WHERE THEY LIVE: on the ground in semiarid areas of sub-Saharan Africa

STATUS: least concern

AND: they have specific warning calls for different predators

IT'S LARRY!

NOT THAT SPECIFIC

YELLOW-THROATED MARTEN
South and east Asia's colorful little killer

TIGERS AREN'T THE ONLY STRIKING BLACK-AND-GOLD COLORED carnivores. There's also the equally arresting yellow-throated marten — and it's just as much a top predator. It comes from the same family as badgers, weasels, and wolverines — animals well known for being fierce and fearless. On its own, a marten will take on something like a rabbit or a pheasant, but when hunting with a partner, as it often does, it will gladly tackle a small deer.

TIGER

Yellow-throated martens live in a range of habitats, from tropical swamps in Indonesia to high mountains and snowy forests in the Himalayas and China. In the south, they are just as willing to eat a mango as a mouse, but in their northern ranges they rely on eating musk deer, and have been seen chasing them onto frozen lakes where the martens' small size and claws give them an advantage. The deer slips and falls and . . . it's all over. Fierce, fearless, *and* smart. The trouble is that as musk deer numbers drop due to hunting by humans, so too do the numbers of yellow-throated martens.

SIZE: as big as a big pet cat

WHAT THEY EAT: just about everything – even sneaky bites of a tiger's kill

WHERE THEY LIVE: from Afghanistan in the west to Korea and Indonesia in the east

STATUS: least concern

AND: they can produce a stinky smell to defend themselves

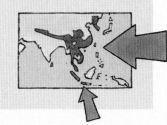

33

GIANT KANGAROO RAT
The Californian critter with a lot of bounce

SOMETIMES ANIMALS ARE NAMED AFTER OTHER ANIMALS. There are kangaroos and there are rats. There are also rat kangaroos and kangaroo rats. Rat kangaroos are small wallaby-like marsupials that look a bit like rodents, and kangaroo rats are small rodents that hop around like wallabies. The rat kangaroos are in Australia, and the kangaroo rats live in the hot, dry deserts of the United States and Mexico.

KANGAROO

RAT

RAT
KANGAROO

KANGAROO
RAT

The giant kangaroo rat is the biggest of the twenty or so kangaroo rat species, all of which are perfectly suited to surviving the tough conditions of the desert. They spend most of their time alone in their burrows, only emerging for a few hours at night to gather food. Unfortunately, owls, rattlesnakes, kit foxes, and coyotes are also out at night gathering food. This is when those long, kangaroo-like legs come in handy. A giant kangaroo rat can leap six and a half feet and change direction in an instant, leaving the predator pouncing on a patch of sand.

Not all the food kangaroo rats gather at night is eaten right away. Kangaroo rats have pocketty pouches on their cheeks for carrying extra food back to their burrows to be stored for later. There might be a few burrows in an area — or hundreds — each one the center of a home territory about half the size of a tennis court. However, the desert needed for all those territories is disappearing fast. The giant kangaroo rat is now restricted to a tiny fraction of the habitat it used to bounce around in. Farms, houses, and energy companies are all expanding into its Californian desert home. **Tough conditions indeed.**

CHEEKY STORAGE

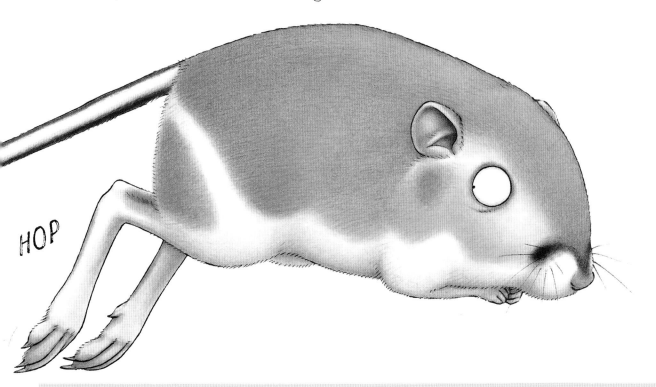

HOP

SIZE: as big as a small guinea pig (with a long tail)

WHAT THEY EAT: seeds, mostly

WHERE THEY LIVE: a few tiny patches of grassy desert in the southwest United States

STATUS: endangered

AND: they drum their feet on the ground as a warning signal

RIBBON SEAL
Rarely seen seal of the icy north Pacific

WHAT A STUNNING CREATURE THE RINGED SEAL IS. IT'S CERTAINLY THE most eye-catching of all the seals and sea lions. And probably one of the most dramatically patterned of any mammal. Such a shame then that hardly anyone has ever heard of it. Perhaps that's because hardly anyone has ever studied it. There's a lot about the ribbon seal we don't know.

We *do* know that they live in the cold far north and that males are darker than females. We know young seals stay with their mothers for just four weeks before they go off on their own.

We know they are deep divers and fast swimmers and that out of water, they move about with a sliding, one-flipper-at-a-time walk, rather than the usual two-flippered bounce of other seals.

LIKE THIS

NOT LIKE THIS

SLIDING WALK

All this we've learned from observations done during the winter and spring when the seals are sitting out on the maze of broken sea ice at the edge of the Arctic. After that, they are harder to follow. It seems that in the summer months they simply swim around in the open ocean, rarely going anywhere near land. But we don't know for sure. Just like we don't know why they have bigger internal organs than other seals or why they have a strange air sack over one side of their ribs. Perhaps it's used to stay afloat all summer. Who knows? **But studied or unstudied they're still stunning.**

SIZE: like a slightly short, fat man – swimming

WHAT THEY EAT: shrimp, squid, and fish

WHERE THEY LIVE: the Bering, Okhotsk, and Chukchi seas in the north Pacific and Arctic oceans

STATUS: data deficient. Hardly surprising

AND: the weight of a newborn pup doubles during its first four weeks

MOUNTAIN TAPIR
Shy herbivore of the equatorial Andes

TAPIRS ARE CURIOUS CREATURES – THEIR CLOSEST RELATIVES ARE rhinos and horses, but with their short trunky noses, there's a bit of elephant about them as well. Tapirs use these handy flexible snouts for finding food and for feeding themselves the food that they find. There are four tapir species: the Malayan tapir lives in Southeast Asia; Baird's tapir, the lowland tapir, and the mountain tapir all live in Central and South America. They are ancient animals and haven't changed much in twenty million years.

MALAYAN TAPIR

BAIRD'S TAPIR

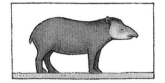
LOWLAND TAPIR

MOUNTAIN TAPIR

The mountain tapir is the smallest and hairiest of the four. Its other, rather apt, name is the woolly tapir. They have short, thick fur to keep themselves warm in the forest uplands where the temperature can fall below freezing. Like all tapirs, the calves are born with a mottled pattern of pale dots and dashes to help them hide in the mottled pattern of dots and dashes of sunlight on the forest floor.

And hiding is a good thing — because the mountain tapir is in danger of extinction. It is hunted for meat and its forest is being cut down. Another twenty million years is looking unlikely. So even though mountain tapirs are strong, fast, agile, and good swimmers, **hiding is probably the way to go.**

SIZE: big pig–sized

WHAT THEY EAT: leaves, grasses, and fruit

WHERE THEY LIVE: cloud forest of the Andes mountains in Colombia, Ecuador, and possibly northern Peru

STATUS: endangered

AND: a possible fifth species was discovered in 2013, but it's not clear if it's just a little lowland tapir

AND ANOTHER THING: mountain tapirs can stay hidden underwater for several minutes and poke their stumpy trunks into the air to stay down even longer

SYRIAN BROWN BEAR
A brown bear that doesn't live in Syria

BROWN BEARS ARE NOT LESSER SPOTTED ANIMALS. THEY ARE among the most well-known creatures on earth. From the mighty grizzly to the long-suffering three that had to put up with Goldilocks, they are definitely ultra A-list celebrities. They are everywhere. Even sitting on our beds.

GRIZZLY

ATLAS

However, the brown bear is not one type of animal. There are, perhaps, fourteen different sorts of brown bear — or subspecies, as they are known. And some of those subspecies are quite *un*-known. If we think that brown bears generally are common we might not realize that individual types of brown bear could be rare — but some are. The Himalayan brown bear is critically endangered. The Atlas bear and the Mexican grizzly are already extinct.

PAPA

The Syrian brown bear is a brown bear that lives in dwindling patches of mountain forest in Turkey, southern Russia, Georgia, Armenia, Azerbaijan, Iraq, and Iran. Sadly, the Syrian brown bear is no longer found in Syria — though it might be hanging on in next-door Lebanon. It was the bear of the Bible but there are no bears in Israel, Palestine, or Egypt anymore. All over their range their numbers are falling. So the next time you pick up your teddy, spare a thought for the Syrian brown bear — **the unknown, well-known bear.**

SIZE: as big as a small bear (but that's still nearly three times the weight of your average *human papa*)

WHAT THEY EAT: just about anything

WHERE THEY LIVE: undisturbed mountain areas from Turkey to southern Russia, and the Middle East

STATUS: vulnerable

AND: they are the smallest and palest of the brown bears

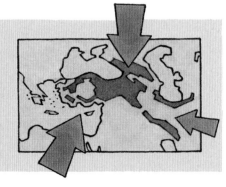

RINGTAIL CAT

Little carnivore once called the miner's cat

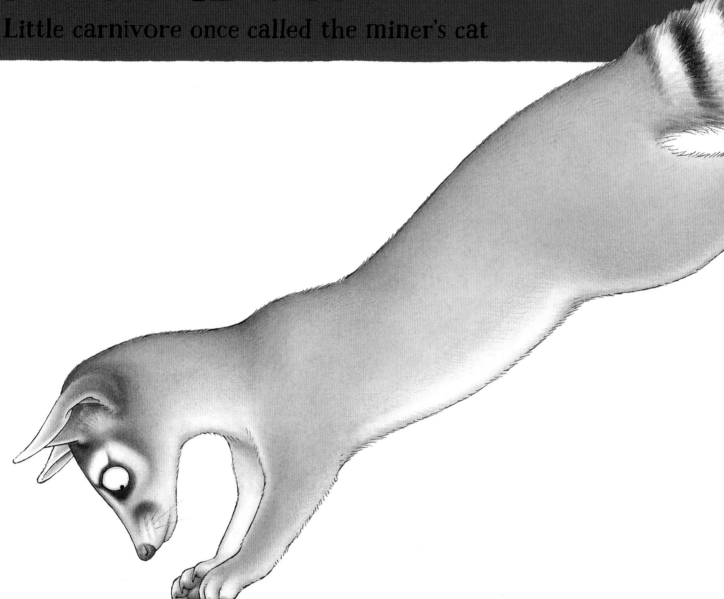

SIZE: as big as a small pet cat

WHAT THEY EAT: frogs, rodents, rabbits, birds, fruit, lizards, flowers, honey

WHERE THEY LIVE: dry rocky woodland near water in Mexico and the southwest United States

I THINK I'M ABOUT TO CROAK

STATUS: least concern

AND: their nearest relative is the very similar cacomistle from Central America

AND ANOTHER THING: the ringtail is the state animal of Arizona

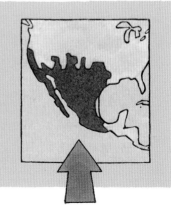

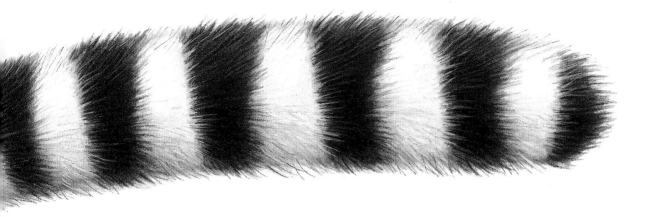

JED SMILED. HE'D HAD A GOOD DAY. THERE'D BEEN A FEW flakes of gold in his pan and he had a notion that if he got that big rock shifted there'd be a lot more waiting for him tomorrow. He leaned his pick and shovel against the rough plank side of his hut and went in. It was already getting dark so he figured on seeing his cat sometime soon.

He reckoned his luck changed when that stripy-tailed critter moved in. For a start, those pesky mice and rats were gone. And up here, alone in the Black Mountains, he liked the company — even if his new friend only woke up at night. A passing prospector told him it wasn't a real cat, that it was something called a ringtail — some sort of relative to a racoon.

Great climbers, the man had said, special back feet that can turn right around so the ringtail can hold on coming down. Jed had seen that sure enough. There was no place in his ramshackle home the cat couldn't get to. And agile? With his own eyes he'd seen the darn thing turn a cartwheel chasing a moth.

He knew ringtails lived in the rocky canyons and hillsides where he and the others miners scratched a living. The ringtails made dens in the caves and among the boulders above the stream. But this one seemed content enough in the little wooden box Jed had made for him. As Jed lit the lamp he saw the pointy nose and bright eyes of his friend. "Hello, cat," said the miner.

HUT

BLACK MOUNTAINS

CARTWHEELING CAT

RINGTAIL CAT

MANED WOLF
The dog with legs like a deer

THE MANED WOLF'S NICKNAME IS THE FOX-ON-STILTS. But it's not a fox. It's not even a wolf. Nor is it that closely related to either foxes or wolves. Just look at it. It's taller than the biggest true wolf yet less than half its weight. And it doesn't hunt in big moose-chasing packs like wolves either. It hunts alone. Those lanky legs are for stalking silently through the long grass and for leaping upon its little-animal prey. Those big ears are for hearing the scurrying sounds of little-animal-prey feet.

WOLF APPLE

WOLF

Having said that, it isn't all about eating other animals — half the maned wolf's diet is fruit and vegetables. There's even a local fruit called the wolf apple because the maned wolf likes it so much. Hardly ferocious. Can you imagine a howling pack of true wolves chasing down a banana? No. This not-a-wolf is not like those other wolves. It is a timid and gentle creature.

The maned wolf is actually a type of wild dog — but because it's called a wolf, people treat it like a wolf. In the past, it was accused of attacking sheep. And even now farmers shoot them for stealing chickens. **It's tough being a dog in wolf's clothing.**

SIZE: roughly greyhound dog–sized, but with even longer legs

WHAT THEY EAT: rodents, rabbits, birds, frogs, and fruit

WHERE THEY LIVE: open grass-land with scattered trees and bushes in central South America

STATUS: near threatened. Their habitat is turning from grassland into farmland

AND: their woof is called a roar-bark – sort of "rrrrrowf"

45

GERENUK

SIZE: skinny llama or super-skinny small pony

WHAT THEY EAT: leaves, buds, flowers, and fruit

WHERE THEY LIVE: open scrubby grassland in northeast Africa

STATUS: near threatened

AND: there are two gerenuk species – northern and southern

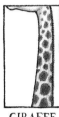

GIRAFFE

G IRAFFES ARE NOT THE ONLY ANIMALS THAT HAVE LEARNED HOW to nibble the taller trees and bushes. Gerenuks and dibatags are long-legged, long-necked antelopes that have figured out the same trick. And if they can't get to the leaves with long necks alone they will stand upright on their back legs, resting their front legs on lower branches, to reach higher.

Both are territorial animals, living in home areas of a few square miles. Say, from the size of Hyde Park in London to as big as Central Park in New York. Males will fight other males who wander into their patch. But there are no fences or signs to show where one territory ends and another begins, so how do you mark where the borders are? With poop, of course.

Like most antelopes, as well as using scent, gerenuks and dibatags use dung to mark out their territories. It tells other gerenuks and dibatags that this bit of bushland is taken. Dibatags always poop in the same places, creating large "dung piles." Gerenuks poop all over the place.

Those graceful long necks, so good for reaching the tastiest green leaves, have made the gerenuks and dibatags amongst the most elegant of all antelopes. They are also good for keeping their noses a long way away from all the poop!

DIBATAG

SIZE: like a big greyhound with an extra-long neck

WHAT THEY EAT: leaves and buds

WHERE THEY LIVE: dry sandy areas of scrub and grass in Ethiopia and Somalia

STATUS: vulnerable – owing to hunting, drought, war, and no protected areas to shelter in

AND: if startled, they'll run off at a dignified trot, with head held high on an arching neck and tail sticking up like a flag

ALTAI ARGALI
Mongolia's monster sheep

YOU HEAR THE SHARP CRACK BEFORE YOU SPOT THE CREATURES THAT made it. The sound echoes around the bleak brown peaks and dusty hills in front of you. Now you see them — on the slope opposite — a herd of about twenty animals that look like sheep. But they can't be sheep, can they? They're way too big. More like ponies — ponies with enormous curling horns.

As you watch, two of these giants are facing off, standing still, almost ten feet apart. Suddenly they rear up onto their back legs and totter toward each other, gathering speed as they go. At the last moment they lower their shoulders and slam their heads together. A second later you hear the same echoing crack you heard a minute ago.

These are Altai argalis, the biggest of all sheep, and their massive twisting horns are the heaviest of all horns. One set of horns can weigh more than 44 pounds. No wonder you can hear them crash together from across the valley. It's those horns that have made the Altai argali famous — famous with hunters that is. Horns make great trophies. And when it comes to hunting, the bigger the trophy the better. A hunter will pay big

money to shoot something with horns like the Altai argali has. Some say the money helps the local community. Some say the argalis are too few to shoot. Listen up, the next sharp crack you hear could be from a rifle.

BAA

SIZE: as big as a tall Shetland pony

WHAT THEY EAT: grass and herbs

WHERE THEY LIVE: dry, open slopes of the Altai Mountains in Mongolia, China, Kazakhstan, and Russia

STATUS: vulnerable – their numbers are decreasing

AND: the Marco Polo argali has the longest horns, sometimes over 55 inches from tip to tip

CELEBES CRESTED MACAQUE
The monkey with a mohawk

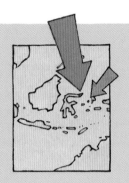

SIZE: three-month-old baby-sister size

WHAT THEY EAT: mostly fruit, but also leaves and seeds, eggs, bugs, and frogs

WHERE THEY LIVE: the northern tip of Sulawesi and neighboring Bacan in Indonesia

STATUS: critically endangered

AND: you say macaque like ma-cack

AND ANOTHER THING: they have bright pink bottoms

BEING A CRITICALLY ENDANGERED ANIMAL CAN BE COMPLICATED. THE CELEBES crested macaque is also called the Sulawesi crested macaque — which is confusing, until you discover that Celebes and Sulawesi are names for exactly the same island in Indonesia. It's also called the black-crested macaque and the black-crested ape. But it's not an ape, it's a macaque.

Macaques are small to medium-sized monkeys often with short or no tails. After humans, they are the most widespread primate, ranging from Gibraltar to Japan. Like most macaques, crested Celebes are active during the day and spend most of the time on the ground, hanging around in extended family groups, looking for food and looking after each other. At night they sleep safely in the trees. Which doesn't sound complicated at all.

But then there's its status. Celebes crested macaques are regarded as crop-raiding pests by farmers, and their rain forest home is under attack from miners and loggers. They are caught for the illegal pet trade and they are even hunted to put on the menu for special occasions and holidays.

GIBRALTAR (BARBARY) MACAQUE

JAPANESE MACAQUE

PET MACAQUE

So in their natural habitat on Sulawesi, their numbers are dropping — alarmingly. There were maybe 25,000 in 1980 — now, perhaps 5,000. However, over on the island of Bacan, where they were introduced in 1867, there could be as many as 100,000. So, problematically, where Celebes crested macaques are meant to be, they are facing extinction, but where they are not meant to be, there are oodles of them. So are they endangered or not? **It's complicated.**

GLOSSARY

Adapt: to become more suited to living in your habitat

Aerial: in the air above the ground

Arid: dry or desert-like. An area with little or no rainfall

Barnacles: small shellfish that stick to hard surfaces like rocks and ships' hulls and whales!

Camouflage: patterns and colors that blend in with the surroundings

Canine teeth: the pointy teeth on either side of the front four flat ones. Long and sharp in cats and dogs

Canopy: the leafy part of a tree

Carnivore: an animal that eats other animals

Cloud forest: tropical mountain forest so high it is in the clouds

Drought: a very long time without rain

Equatorial: near the equator

Extinct: no more of that type of animal left alive. The end of a species

Female: girls, women, and moms — animal or otherwise

Grubs: the caterpillar-like stage of insects

Herbivore: an animal that eats plants

Lateral hooves: a second pair of hooves behind the main two at the front

Lichen: dry, crusty, or mossy-looking form of fungus

Lowland: not up mountains

Male: boys, men, and dads — animal or otherwise

Mammal: a warm-blooded and usually furry animal that feeds its young with milk. Dolphins and whales are mammals. But they're not furry.

Marine: about or from the sea

Marsupial: a mammal that carries its developing babies in a pouch. Kangaroos and koalas are marsupials

Nectar: a sweet, sticky liquid made by flowers

Nocturnal: mostly active at night

Poaching: hunting animals illegally

Pollen: the fine powdery stuff made by flowers which is needed to make seeds and fruit, and so, baby plants

Predator: an animal that hunts other animals and eats them

Primate: a monkey, ape, or human

Prospector: someone who searches for valuable minerals — like gold

Rain forest: lush forest growing in the wetter parts of the world

Savannah: open grassland in tropical areas, with few trees

Scent: a perfume-like substance animals use to mark territory or attract a mate

Scrub: an area of bushes and small trees

Shrew: a small, pointy-nosed, insect-eating mammal

Species: the individual variety of an animal

Status: a grading of animals based on how likely they are to become extinct

Sub-Saharan: south of the Sahara desert in Africa

Termite: wood-eating, ant-like insects that live in large colonies

Tick: tiny blood-sucking creature related to spiders

Trophy: a souvenir of a kill to be mounted on a wall — often the stuffed head and horns

Tusks: extra-long teeth sticking out of the mouth like in walruses and elephants

Wallaby: one of a number of marsupials that looks like a small kangaroo

Zoolesserspottedology: a word I just made up, meaning the study of unfamiliar animals

STATUS: The status entries in this book are based on a list of threatened species put together by the International Union for Conservation of Nature. This IUCN Red List, as it is called, is the most thorough register of information on the conservation situation of the planet's plants and animals. Nearly 64,000 species have been evaluated and given a mark indicating how near to extinction they are. This grading, or status, goes like this:

- **Data deficient:** not enough is known to make a judgment
- **Least concern:** no need to worry at present
- **Near threatened:** likely to be endangered in the future
- **Vulnerable:** likely to be endangered soon
- **Endangered:** at risk of becoming extinct
- **Critically endangered:** extremely high risk of becoming extinct
- **Extinct in the wild:** only survives in captivity
- **Extinct:** gone

And finally . . .

Whether you're least concern or critically endangered, a big-name lion or a little-name loris, whether you're called a macaque or an ape, you deserve to have a home and you deserve your name to be known.

So what's the name of your favorite monkey? Still not sure? Well here's another one to choose from. It's a pity there isn't room for a full entry — but this book is already as big as it can be!

REALLY? THIS IS ALL I GET?

GEE'S GOLDEN LANGUR